THE [MAN]UAL

Junior Ziegler

Nimanore Publishing
Chicago, Illinois

All rights reserved. No part of this publication may be reproduced, distributed or transmitted in any form or by any means, without prior written permission.

**Nimanore Publishing
Chicago, IL**

All Scripture quotations, unless otherwise indicated, are taken from The Holy Bible, **English Standard Version**®, (ESV®), copyright © 2001 by Crossway, a publishing ministry of Good News Publishers. Used by permission. All rights reserved. Scripture quotations marked NKJV are taken from the New King James Version. Copyright ©1979, 1980, 1982 by Thomas Nelson, Inc. Used by permission. All rights reserved. Scripture quotations marked NLT are taken from the Holy Bible, New Living Translation, copyright © 1996. Used by permission of Tyndale House Publishers, Inc., Wheaton Illinois, 60189. All rights reserved. Scripture marked NIV are taken from the Holy Bible, New International Version®, (NIV®), copyright © 1973, 1978, 1984 by International Bible Society. Used by permission of Zondervan. All rights reserved.

The [Man]ual / Junior Ziegler. -- 1st ed.
ISBN 979-8-218-25512-1

Nicole,

Thanks for pushing and supporting my leadership, especially when I didn't model these pages.

Dedicated to my dad.
You live this and more.

Contents

Introduction……………………………………..…..1

Chapter 1: When We Lost Something……..……….…5

Chapter 2: A Word Redefined…………….………..…15

Chapter 3: Difference Between Boys & Men…….…....27

Chapter 4: Vision Wins…………..…..…………..……39

Chapter 5: Thermostats & Thermometers…...………..51

Chapter 6: Home Protection…….…..…………..……67

Chapter 7: Deepen Your Roots……..…………..……..85

Conclusion……………………………...….………..101

Introduction

A Lost Definition

I recently heard a frustrated woman voluntarily announce, "I'm single because there are no good men left." While it could be more likely she's single for a slew of other reasons…her sentiment is echoed by many.

I beg to differ. Maybe good men are becoming endangered… but they aren't extinct, far from it.

The trouble is, we struggle to identify just what exactly a good man looks like. Often, the pretty-boy selfie kings fill the social media timelines while the chauvinistic brutes make the headlines with cases of abuse. The men who fill the space in between aren't as post-able, therefore they feel lost to the masses. In a social media driven world, this has created confusion over what a good man actually looks like.

To add to the confusion, manhood has been placed under the microscope, maybe for good reason. Patriarchal society and toxic masculinity have been confronted…it's fine, real men welcome a challenge. Though as society has challenged and in some cases deconstructed—manhood has been all but cancelled.

The "Y" chromosome is almost politically incorrect.

Testosterone, the very drive that built society, protected families and forged new paths is also the same drive that raped women, attacked the innocent and sparked wars. In an effort to end the later, we can easily neuter the former.

With the intention to end toxic masculinity, we spread it.

Just like itching poison ivy to relieve the pain only spreads the toxins, neutering manhood to end toxicity only spreads the very thing we're trying to kill.

However, as perceptions shift and definitions challenged—an integral thread of society is beginning to unravel.

What is manhood?

A question no society in world history has wrestled with more than today. Yet this fundamental question, that if left unanswered, will collapse communities like a house of cards.

As this question remains unanswered, marketers are cashing in. Next time a sporting event is on TV, pay attention to the commercials. When a male dominated audience exists, advertisers will tell the men how to be a man.

"Drive this truck, you'll look more like a man."

"Drink this beer, you're a man."

"Take this magical blue pill, and you're going to be able to do more of what makes you feel like a man."

Marketers ingeniously, yet sadly are selling masculinity to men, because men are confused. The question remains unanswered. What does it look like to be a man?

To speak into the single lady's concern—real men still exist, they're just not busy snapping selfies to keep up with an image-driven, neutered society. They're also not out cheating and abusing.

They're doing far less postable activities. You can find them sporting blue collars, white collars, rednecks. They're coaching little leagues, working desk jobs, rewiring buildings. They're the men who wake up each day and fill the space between the trending soy-boy tiktoks and the brutal headlines. They're men who pick up after the deadbeats, and don't crave the praise of a comment section for it.

Maybe they're endangered, but they're certainly not extinct.

Instead of waving goodbye, they deserve to be studied. Because when they are, there is something you'll find that all good men have in common. It's far more simple than expected (it's why this handbook is shorter).

Maybe testosterone need not be apologized for. For good men have and do channel it to bless, protect, and bring peace. Maybe it's time to get back to the basics of manhood.

Lets strip away the sales pitches, products & politically correct definitions. Lets discover the core of manhood. Let's reclaim an integral thread of society, and lets do so in such a way that exposes "toxic manhood" for what it is, not manhood. Welcome to the short manual, I think you'll find power in the simplicity.

Chapter One

When We Lost Something

Philadelphia, PA, 1850s. An orange hue glow grows on the horizon slowly waking the city of brotherly love. In a few decades, this city will have trolley cars dropping off factory workers introducing a new public transportation. All of that is brewing—but not yet realized. Instead, Philadelphia's 30+ streets, mostly named after trees, will soon fill with wagons, horses, and crowds of commuters.[1]

Sawdust floor butcher shops unlock their doors. Family-run drug stores with soda fountains flip their sign to open. Straight razor barbers ready their chairs. It's a simpler life, though it's all becoming more complicated.

Like most major U.S. cities at this time, Philadelphia is experiencing a population surge.[2] Thanks to the industrial revolution, Urban areas now have more to offer—factory work

The [Man]ual 5

which included a steady income and often a higher paycheck than the generational family business could offer.

In many ways, the boom of factories brought families an easier way of living. Products were now far more readily available to the masses making home life easier. Andrew Carnegie's steel mills would make long distant transportation an option for the average middle-class family.

Even more than the ease of life, the Industrial Revolution brought opportunities to men for serious money to be made in production.

Though great progress, something precious was lost.

The Great Trade

Before the Industrial Revolution, men provided products, services, and business as almost an extension of the family. The family name was often tied to the product the father produced, hence why some family names include the trade (i.e. My family name is Ziegler which, from what I hear, comes from the clay tile roof. Apparently I come from a family of clay tile roofers). The family trade was near and dear to the family— often families were identified by their product/service.

For the average pre-Industrial Revolution family, boys grew up watching dad sacrifice to deliver a service or create a product. For many boys, upon reaching puberty, rather than being sent to a classroom dominated by mainly female instructors— boys went to work with dad learning the family trade. There was daily discipline of the early mornings to make the most of the sunlight. All day they would learn the craft from their old man. They would experience firsthand the cost of an earned dollar and the value of sweat and that feeling of a solid days worth of work.

For a father, it was simply part of the job to cast vision for the younger generation. To pass on their craft, to instill pride of what previous generations have taught. To be a man was to teach the art of business to young minds — how to make a product/service as well as how to sell that product/service.

Though running a family business was at times playing with poverty, there was a sense of beauty in it. Sons would learn how to work like a man. They would pick up from their father how to talk like a man and how to relate to other men. They would shoulder the duty of providing like a man. This was, in essence, the duty of the husband/father.

The Industrial Revolution ushered in a new way of life. While it brought many conveniences making everyday life more bearable, the role of man started to shift.

Hiring factories offered larger, steadier paychecks. It was seemingly a no-brainer. But it might have come at a cost that few, if any, would have accounted for.

To make a better immediate living, a father could sell his day to a mass production factory. Men could sell their day instead of their goods. While this would entail long hours away from home, it would afford a better life for those under his roof.

Unintentionally men traded their craft, generational mentoring, family time, and the family business for a larger, steadier income. While the short-term effects yielded great benefits, the long-term effects weren't considered.

The trade men made, left the next generation of boys with a void. Since child labor laws had not yet been implemented, many boys went to factories to work menial jobs. Instead of spending their days with dad catching vision and learning manhood, boys could also bring home a paycheck.

In other cases, boys were sent for more schooling. Sure, there were and are great benefits in more education, but there was a loss of time with dad to learn how to become and navigate manhood.

As the Industrial Revolution brought great convenience, something precious yet unaccounted for was lost. The values and clear, simple definition of manhood tragically became ever so slightly blurred with each generation.

And the effects are felt today.

The Loss of Friendship

Recent studies show that a great "male friendship recession" is plaguing our society.[3] Men have fewer friends than ever before. We find it harder and harder to relate with each other. At least I do.

My wife, who is a far better socialite than me, can go out with her girlfriends for coffee and not think twice. When a guy asks me to get a cup of coffee, maybe I shouldn't—but I feel weird. We're going to go sit at a little bistro table and sip coffee at a coffee shop? What are we going to do? Just look at each other? I don't want to do that. I'd rather sit across from my wife, she's far better to look at.

I don't think I'm the only guy that think it's kind of weird.

Allow me to broad-brush genders for a second (I know this could get me cancelled, but I'll wear it as a badge). Most (not all) women make friends face to face. My wife can get coffee with another woman and they'll have a blast and leave the table closer friends not feeling

8   **Junior Ziegler**

awkward in the slightest. It's God's beautiful design.

Most (not all) men are different. We don't want to sit across and stare at another guy's face (unless maybe a cigar is involved or a fire is between us). Instead, we're shoulder to shoulder. Guys tend to grow closer to other guys by working on a project together. I don't want to sit at a little coffee shop bistro table with you, but I'd grow closer to you by swinging a hammer next to you or fishing on a boat with you. I'm not just coming up with stereotypical manly activities, but this is why these actives are stereotypical. Men make friends shoulder to shoulder—accomplishing something together.

Before the Industrial Revolution, men grew closer to their boys by working on the family business together. Men in a typical community had more friendships and contacts because the community family businesses often intersected.

As the factories moved in, men mainly did menial work with fewer men around them. There was no need for creative brainstorming and partnerships. Relationships and contacts just weren't as necessary. Men still chilled and grilled on the rare day off—but the communal shoulder to shoulder projects ceased to be a necessary part of life.

The Redefinition of Success

Not only were friendships lost, but the definition of success for men was redefined.

As men closed their family businesses to migrate to factories—success took on a new meaning. For the generations before them, success entailed the advancement of their family product/service. Success was also tied to the next generation learning the trade and catching the vision.

As men clocked in for their shifts at their new factory, their father's definition of success was no longer relevant. A steadier bigger paycheck was dangled in front of them. They could now live better than ever and provide more income for their than their dads provided for them. The digits on the paycheck became the definition of success.

It's no secret that today success is mainly defined by earning power. However, success was far more holistic before the Industrial Revolution. Family dynamics, community connection, and friendship was an integral part of success.

Fumbling the Handoff

It's not just men struggling, the future men—the boys. Today, girls overwhelmingly account for the top GPA in schools across The United States.[4] Almost one in four boys in school are categorized as having a "developmental disability".[5] Boys are struggling in school.

Woodworking, machining, and many other male dominated trades have been disappearing from the school system. Male students seem to be acting out all the more.

As girls dominate the top 10% of GPA, boys dominate the suspension rate.[6]

Before the Industrial Revolution it was seen as the father's job to guide a boy through boyhood and into manhood. He as the primary discipliner and vision caster. Today, that responsibility has been unfairly placed on the school system, and the results are a crisis.

Transition from boyhood to manhood has been effectively fumbled.

It's Not Too Late

I don't intend to sound the alarms. Our crisis selling media does that enough. I'm merely pointing out, our society is finding and feeling first-hand the detrimental effects of losing the definition of manhood. Boys are confused as to where to aim their drive, often landing them in juvenile detention schools and programs.

Men are experiencing a recession of friendship, confusing men all the more on just what it is to be a man. Society is starving for what it lost so long ago. But it can be recovered. The silver lining—real, good men will stand out and impact this world more than ever before. This is no time to hold a funeral, it's a moment such as this great men take the opportunity before them. But first, we must discover what exactly it means to be a man.

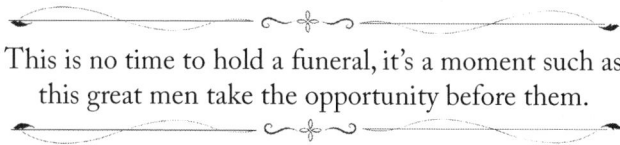

This is no time to hold a funeral, it's a moment such as this great men take the opportunity before them.

Chapter Challenge

What are some lessons you wish the men in your life would've taught you as you grew up?

Where do you see men (yourself included) struggling the most today?

THE {MAN}UAL

14   **Junior Ziegler**

Chapter Two

A Word Redefined

In 1844, George Washington Bush, an African American, together with his white, German wife and five sons left the South to head west—a beautiful land hopefully void of racism. Like other pioneers heading west, Bush and his beautiful family faced extreme hardship from the terrain—hunger, droughts, and illness. Yet, the prospect of having his own family farm pushed them onward.

Upon arriving, the Bush family became the first permanent American settlers in Puget Sound. It seemed as though Bush had provided his dream for his family. Freedom, land, and a clear route to prosper.

The [Man]ual

However, not long after their arrival—the Bush family learned their rights as a black family were denied. Through many dark days and good friends appealing on their behalf, the Bush family was able to keep their land near Puget Sound and farmed with great success.

The story has an even better ending.

As George Washington Bush enjoyed not only freedom but success, he used his wealth to provide more families with the same opportunity his family experienced. Filling wagons with silver dollars, he funded the cross-country trek for many families. Upon their arrival, George would give away full harvests to feed the newcomers.

It's the classic heart-warming story, an underdog pushing through obstacles to success only to turn around and give his success to others. It's a beautiful, yet often untold story.

More than a heartwarming story, it's a story of what manhood is. George Washington Bush not only provided those under his roof with food, he provided opportunity and a better future. He then saw it as his duty to provide the same for others.

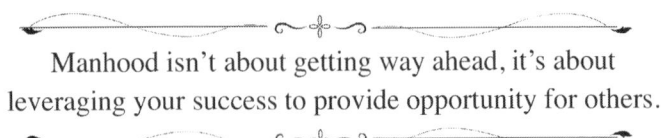

Manhood isn't about getting way ahead, it's about leveraging your success to provide opportunity for others.

Bush's son Owen took over the family farm in 1866 following his dad's death. Beyond farming, Owen also served in the first Washington State Legislature. Bush descendants farmed that land for over 100 years.

George Washington Bush provided far more than a paycheck.[7]

An Oversimplified Definition

Of all the changes (good and bad) that the Industrial Revolution brought, the biggest change was the redefinition of the word *provision*. Pre-Industrial Revolution, provision carried greater meaning. Today, *provision*, for most has a simple definition. This oversimplification of one word has led to tragic confusion over what it means and looks like to be a man.

Case in point, when you see the word provision—what's the first idea that comes to mind? For most, including myself, we think of money.

So if the average man off the street is asked, "Do you provide for your family." Most will emphatically answer "Yes!" They work a job, receive a paycheck, and put food on the table. To provide is to feed mouths and clothe kids.

Believe it or not, it's that oversimplified way of thinking that is leading to today's major problems. We've almost depleted manhood to simply mean "sugar daddy". "Just bring home the bacon, here's a pat on the head—you're a 'man." That's all manhood is? Also, what about my paralyzed friend in a wheelchair? His earning power is severely limited. Does that therefore mean his manhood is limited too? Of course not!

Our current simplified view of provision sucks. We lost a really good definition, and it needs to be reclaimed. To do that, let's explore the ancient definition.

An Ancient Definition

There are many different views about the Bible. The goal of this book is not to shove Scripture down your throat. However, aside from the fact that I'm a pastor, I do think you'll find Scripture's definition of the word "provision" interesting. Whether you believe Scripture is from God or not, we can all agree it's ancient. It only makes sense, to reclaim an old definition requires finding original uses of the word.

So for a moment, let's use Scripture for definition purposes. Paul of Tarsus wrote this roughly 2,000 years ago to a younger guy he was mentoring...

*If anyone does not **provide** for his relatives, and especially for members of his household, he has denied the faith and is worse than an unbeliever...[8]*

Many people have used this to discuss welfare, if a man is sitting around making babies and sucking on the teat of the government—he's not being a true man. While that's certainly a discussion worth having, it goes to show how oversimplified our definition of *provide* has become. The reality is, a man can put a feast on the table each night, clothe his kids in Gucci, and still not be providing for his family.

Wealthy homes are often dysfunctional. Financial provision is only a small piece of the pie.

To understand the ancient use, let's dissect that verse a little more. First, notice the male pronouns used. Paul is specifically addressing men and those under their roof.

Since Paul wrote this originally in Greek, the word he used for *provide* is a word most non-Greeks can't read (προνοέω). This word appears in many other places of literature, and when it does it's often translated as "to have vision for, to care for, to teach". The ancient understanding of *provide* meant something far more than a financial providing sugar-daddy.

Pre-Industrial revolution, to be a man meant to be a vision-caster, passion-passer. If you're a man, you're more than some sugar daddy—you were designed to provide far more—leadership for those under your roof.

Excuses

It's here where I hear a lot of guys begin to make excuses. We'll look at a healthy roof, a family where the dad is exhibiting healthy, solid leadership— and to make ourselves feel better we'll peg them as having it easier. "Well, his wife is easier to get along with." "His kids are far more easygoing than my kids." In other words, "That guy doing better than me has a better context and easier roof than I have…"

This is the part of the book many guys will close. "Alright Junior, I picked up your old-looking book on manhood but page 19 is as far as I'm going. Congrats, your book is now a coaster." I get it.

Those of us guys who are struggling to step up get very sensitive. Deep down we know we're supposed to step up. We know we're supposed to provide more than a paycheck, but the wife doesn't make it easy, and the kids don't listen. So to read a book like this can feel like you're just being piled on.

Keep reading…

My wife is one of the most independent women I've ever met. It's incredible to watch her. She'll sign up for a marathon 3 weeks before the race and run it. She'll go camping, by herself! When we make camp, she wants to be the one to make the fire to cook. When we snowboard, I tumble down the hill and she goes off jumps. She's a type-A, independent woman. I knew what I was marrying—it's awesome.

To be candid with you, it used to bother me at times. If she was more dainty, maybe I'd feel a little bit stronger sometimes.

It's not like she's masculine, she's just so dang independent. She's a firecracker, I'm a cigar. I'm far more chill than my wife, and you'd experience that within 5 minutes of hanging out with us.

So naturally, at the beginning of our marriage, it was a struggle. Why do I need to step up? She's got everything under control. Why lead? Look at her!

My passivity hurt us. I believe (and so does Nicole) that God made Nicole to desire leadership. My failure to lead wasn't fair to her, nor was it good for my roof. Instead, it slowly bred resentment. I wasn't providing what I was made to provide, and Nicole wasn't receiving what she was designed to desire.

But what am I going to do? You try leading a type-A personality.

One day I realized something. This is just my belief, you might not share it and that's ok. But this conviction reframed my situation. I believe one day I will stand before God. God is going to ask me how I did doing what He created me to do, provide leadership for a girl He blessed me with. No excuses will work.

"Well God, I realize you designed me to lead. And I realize you designed Nicole to deep down desire leadership…but you have to ask her. You put too much TNT in her, I could hardly keep up with her so I just decided to embrace the sugar-daddy role and bring home a paycheck (even though she made more than me). Ask her."

Here's why it won't work—it didn't work in the Garden of Eden.

Go back to the first man and woman in the Bible. When Adam and Eve sinned, Adam was the one God looked for to answer for the family.

When Adam stood before God, he deflected to Eve. Adam had the cojones to say, "It was the woman you gave me. Ask her!" The deflection didn't work.

A lot of husbands live their lives like the first man, Adam. We might want to step up. We might want to lead…we might feel guilty when we see other guys building healthy homes. But we live deflecting to the woman that God gave us. "I'd lead, but it's her…I'm just doing what I can…"

I believe God designed you and knows you better than you know yourself. He knows exactly what you can handle, and He blessed you with exactly that. Don't take a blessing from God (a woman and children) and point at the blessing as an excuse for not doing what you were designed to do.

With blessing comes more responsibility. When we fail at the responsibility part, the blessing becomes a curse.

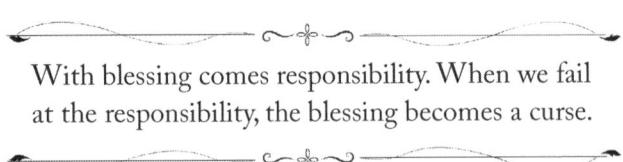

With blessing comes responsibility. When we fail at the responsibility, the blessing becomes a curse.

The best way to develop your leadership is to develop it in your home. Regardless of how successful you are in your career, your leadership never exceeds the health of your roof. Leadership is most tested under the roof—lean into that, your wife only makes you a better leader.

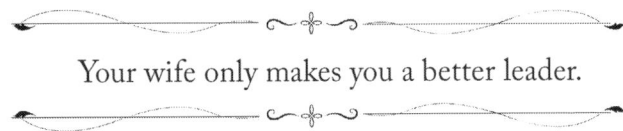

Your wife only makes you a better leader.

Adaptable Definition

One of the main issues of this conversation is there's no recipe for manhood. A recipe would be nice. Do a little of this, add a little of that and voila—you're a B.A. Johnny Bravo! There's no checklist and for good reason. No two roofs are the same. A man providing under one roof is going to look a little different than his neighbor providing under the roof next to him.

For example, I have my type-A wife and three daughters. One of my best friends has a type-B wife with a couple sons. He's a great man, what he's doing to provide for his roof often looks very different than me. Another friend of mine is a bachelor navigating the dating realm and contributing to his community. His manhood looks even more different than ours.

There's no one-shoe fits all recipe for men—all our roofs look different. The application of leadership looks different on the context, but the principle stays the same. You have yourself to discipline, you're walking/talking evidence of your own leadership. The proof of your leadership is in the pudding, and you're the pudding. And if you have a home, team, or staff—you will answer for how you led them as well.

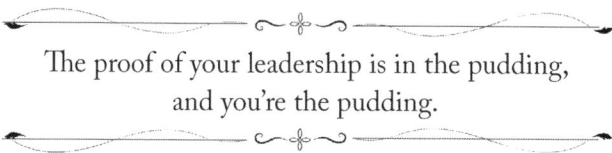

The proof of your leadership is in the pudding, and you're the pudding.

Rather than spending the rest of the pages pumping you up to do stereotypical manly things to "feel" manly and hype up whatever testosterone you have, let's instead unpack what the fundamentals of provision actually look like under your roof.

We'll apply each differently, but the fact of the matter remains—to be a man means to provide. So let's reclaim the holistic definition of *provision* and explore its adaptable application.

24 **Junior Ziegler**

Chapter Challenge

What excuses have you been using to not lead yourself past where you are now?

What excuses have you been using to not lead those under your care?

What's it going to take to lead better tomorrow?

THE {MAN}UAL

26 **Junior Ziegler**

Chapter Three

Difference Between Boys & Men

A rare chill grips the city of New Orleans on January 16, 1972.[9] It was an unseasonably cold day, but to many the chill came from the sidelines of the Tulane Stadium. Surrounded by white jerseys stood a stoic man in a long black coat and iconic fedora. Tom Landry, coach of the Dallas Cowboys, quietly yet confidently watched his team walk over the Miami Dolphins. From this moment forward, Landry would not only sport his championship ring, he would lead his team to another championship and 15 consecutive winning seasons.

For so many, there was an alluring mystique to Tom Landry. His quiet, yet strong leadership was effective—more effective

The [Man]ual 27

than his demonstrative peers. Hate him or love him, Tom could and did make men better on and off the field.

A quote machine, Landry once said—

The job of a football coach is to make men do what they don't want to do, in order to achieve what they've always wanted to be.[10]

I whole heartedly agree with Coach Landry however this job is not just reserved for "football coaches." I would add, the job of every man is to make themselves do what they don't want to do, in order to achieve what they were made to be—a man. The fundamental job of man is to do what he doesn't feel like doing. This is where provision begins.

The truth might be, you aren't where you want to be. You don't have what you want, because you're too undisciplined for it. Many boys stay boys because they can't get this down.

Provision Starts Here

In the words of Michael Scott quoting Rodney Dangerfield, "I get no respect." I've heard far too many guys repeat that idea as an excuse for not leading their roof. Their wife doesn't seem remotely interested in following their leadership. Their kids certainly have no interest in following dad. As a result many guys claim the backseat. I get it. It hurts when nobody wants to follow you. Taking the backseat and not trying to lead is a way to cope. It hurts less if we don't try, right?

Most guys don't try to lead because they don't want to hurt when nobody follows them. But it's deeper than that… They haven't led themselves well.

In many situations, I haven't really blamed the wife or kids for not wanting to follow the man of the house. Why should a self-respecting wife and kids follow an undisciplined leader? Just because you have something between your legs doesn't automatically elevate you in the eyes of those under your roof. Self-discipline is what gives credibility to a leader.

If you're a mess financially, spend whatever you make—why would anyone respect you enough to follow? If you eat whatever, never work out, get off on porn, talk like a sleazy sailor, and claim the corner of your couch— who wants to follow that? Farm animals don't follow the pigs.

Far too many men, who were designed to lead, sit in the backseat of their home stewing in bitterness because not many follow their leadership. Lead yourself first. The proof is in the pudding. If you're crashing your career, crashing your body, crashing your purity, crashing your finances…why would anyone give a man like that the steering wheel? That's as nutty as a Coast Guard lifeboat rescuing a crashed ocean liner and allowing the captain of the crash to drive the survivors back to shore. A man who can't lead himself certainly shouldn't be leading his home. A man will never lead someone further than he's led himself.

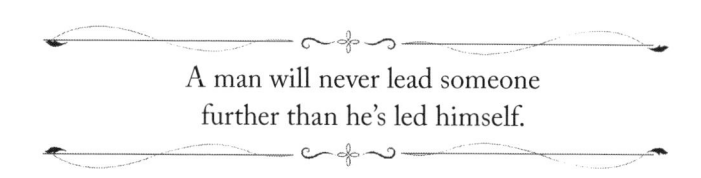

> A man will never lead someone
> further than he's led himself.

Provision starts with self-discipline.

A while back, I sat in an old World War II hanger rehabbed into a camp chapel. It was a fall night, and the little hanger was busting at the seams with about 250 guys. That night, my friend Corey Brooks, a pastor from Chicago's South Side, spoke on discipline. It was a 30 minute beat down that I needed.

At the time, I had been on a 10 year journey of developing my dad bod. I hadn't consistently worked out since high school, I wanted to eat well but my lack of discipline always won out. I realized I lived frustrated. I blamed my eating habits on too many children's snacks in the house. I blamed my lack of working out on having young kids and not being able to get to the gym. Meanwhile, my wife was running at 6am every morning while I slept. She ate a healthy breakfast while I woke up late and downed carbs.

How am I supposed to expect to provide for my wife when she was more disciplined than me?

So that night in the hanger, I made a commitment. For the next year I would be noticeably more disciplined than my strong-independent wife.

To be honest, this sucked.

Many nights this last year, my last question of the day to her was "when will your alarm go off?"

"5:15"

"Frick." So I set my alarm for 5. I have to beat her out of bed. I have to be the first to the gym. I have to sweat more. I have to be first to Scripture. And I have to have a healthier plate at the breakfast table. The lion has to push harder than the lioness, regardless of how strong and disciplined the lioness is.

Within the first 6 months I had lost 20 pounds, but that wasn't my goal. My goal was making my leadership worth following…if I was going to provide for my roof, I first had to lead myself far better.

Don't get me wrong, this wasn't a competition with my wife, though sometimes it's playful to compete about who worked out harder in the morning. Yesterday my wife burned 1700 calories on a long run, so I literally burned 1701 this morning. It's playful fun, but there's a point to it and it's not competitive.

This isn't about outdoing my wife. This is all about making it easier for her to follow my lead. She's strong, independent, and disciplined...I love it, bring it on! Instead of jumping in the backseat, her strength will be my motivation to be even stronger. And our marriage has never been better.

I don't write this to be "the hero." More often than not I am my own villain.

I write this because I understand the pull to take the backseat. I've been back there. My girl knows what she wants and goes after it—it's sexy. I don't mind sitting back—it's more comfortable. Yet this only bred frustration in her and bitterness in me because I was designed to lead and she was designed to desire my leadership.

To lead a roof, you must first lead yourself. To provide for a family, you must first discipline yourself.

As goes the leader, so goes the roof. The leader must be on it. The man can't blame a home that doesn't want to follow lazy leadership.

Nobody's going to follow you simply because of your anatomical make-up. They'll follow you because you lead yourself well. Self-discipline is an absolute credential for leadership.

Be The First To What Many Are Last To

Discipline is seen most when walking toward what most avoid. You want to prove manhood? Forget the truck, beer and blue pill commercials. Look for what most are last to—and be the first to it. Be the first one out of bed. Be the first to sweat. Be the first to take responsibility. Be the first to clean up.

Be last to eat, last to the couch, last to spend money.

In a world racing to be first to pleasure, good men race toward that which most run from. The first step toward being a man is walking toward that which everyone runs from.

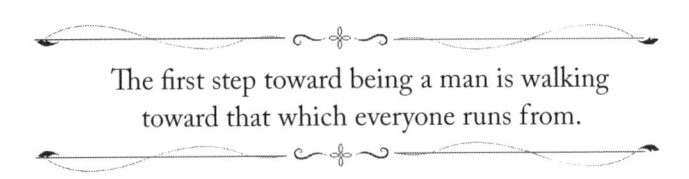

> The first step toward being a man is walking toward that which everyone runs from.

The Difference Between Boys and Men

Watch the news for more than 30 seconds and we are reminded, our world has festering problems, because our world is full of boys who can shave. Self-discipline and self-leadership is the greatest differentiator between boys and men. Men do what boys avoid. Here's how this looks…

- **Men have hard conversations. Boys avoid and allow it to fester.**

As a pastor, I see this plaguing communities. Many homes are homes of egg shell flooring, just one wrong step away from a massive blow up.

The house also has lumps under the rugs from years of sweeping issues underneath. When the kids leave, they don't want to return—who wants to live walking on egg shells and tripping over lumps on the rugs? Unhealthy homes avoid necessary conversation out of fear of awkwardness and conflict. The healthiest homes have a man who doesn't avoid difficult conversations.

- **Men look for avenues to solve. Boys look for platforms to complain.**

Loud mouths are terrible problem solvers. Those who wear their heart on their social media sleeve whining to the world never experience solutions. Gossips only ever compound problems. Boys look for platforms to air opinions and grievances. Men look for problems to solve, and are more than happy to do so under the radar.

- **Men seek growth. Boys seek comfort.**

Boys have an eye for comfort, cutting corners to get the job done quicker, avoiding responsibility for more time on the couch. Boys who do work often work for the reward of simply a paycheck and a pleasure.

Men work for the reward of growth. There's pride in the work. Men are energized by making something better.

- **Men are driven by impact. Boys are driven by attention.**

It's why the woman in the introduction blurted out, "There's no good men." Because the boys are out taking space on timelines with selfies. Boys are more seen, and are driven by it.

Men are driven by impact. Making a real impact is usually quiet work. It's certainly not post-able. It's years of faithfulness to thankless tasks.

Impact drives men, attention drives boys.

- **Men tactfully challenge their spouse. Boys effectively ruin their spouse.**

Give a boy a good woman, he'll ruin her. He'll take backseat, shrink back and frustrate her. His cowardly life will either be contagious to her or force her to be someone she doesn't want to be by stepping up to fill his lack of leadership. Often you can tell who's a boy after a few years of having a woman. Is she better or worse? Boys ruin good women.

On the other hand, give a man a good woman, and he'll only make her better. His leadership and responsibility will clear a lane for her to run even better. His challenges will only grow her. His boldness gives her confidence. His strength (even standing up to her) will give her security and direction. Good men help make great women.

Discipline is a way of life.

Pass It On

When a man leads himself into self-discipline, he provides it to his home by passing it on to his children. A self-disciplined father is in position to provide healthy discipline to his kids. Ephesians 6:4 says—

> *Fathers are to bring up their children with discipline.*

For Christian men, there's no option—they are the main providers of discipline. First, men provide discipline for themselves, and then they provide it for their children.

The insufferable complaints about the next generation have become common rhetoric.

"The next generation is soft."

"The next generation is entitled."

"The next generation is lazy."

I don't disagree with all the complaints—but who's that on? If those complaints are true, who dropped the ball? A generation is a reflection of the provision of the former generation. If this generation struggles with self-discipline—it means discipline wasn't provided by yesterday's fathers.

To be a man is to provide discipline, first for himself and then for his kin. But until he's disciplined, nobody wants what he provides. The rest of this book doesn't really matter, until this chapter happens.

Chapter Challenge

Each Sunday night, imagine a version of yourself 5% more disciplined than you. He ate 5% healthier, he lifted 5% more, he got 5% more work done, he used a screen 5% less.

Beat that version of yourself that week.

Junior Ziegler

Chapter Four

Vision Wins

Detroit, Michigan, 1913. Street cars packed with people cut through town dropping off commuters. There's an electric energy that seems to buzz in the air as urban economy grows. Nobody can put their finger on it, but it feels as though Detroit's best days are just around the corner.

This morning, one of the commuters is a man named Henry who's about to make that feeling a reality. He clinches the stack of papers in his hand tightly while he heads toward the bank. As he cuts through Detroit, Henry doesn't just see the city for what it is today, he sees Detroit's tomorrow and he's convinced he will be a major part of it. This city will be "Motor City." Many of the men walking by will one day work for him.

This morning, Henry signs the papers for what will be the Ford Assembly Line building. Immediately following the purchase, Henry gets to work outfitting the warehouse, prepping it to be filled with workers, car parts, and machinery.

Henry's mission is simple—reduce the manufacture time of a car form 12 hours to under 2 hours. If Henry can pull this off, Ford Motor Company will drastically cut costs making the automobile available to the masses.

The rest is history. American production was revolutionized. Cars litter our streets today.

Here's what didn't happen…

Henry didn't purchase his building, fit it with equipment, fill it with workers, while having no product envisioned. Once people punched in for the day, Henry **did not** gather everyone up and say, "What do ya'll want to make today?"

"The hardware store down the street seems low on wrenches, want to try making that?"

Or…

"I saw a car this weekend, seemed pretty cool. You all want to try to make that?"

That'd be ludicrous. Henry Ford started with his vision and then outfitted his factory and team to accomplish the vision. It would be pure idiocy to have a business, workers, teams and then decide what to produce. That would be backwards.

Tragically, most men are doing this with their lives and homes. There's no vision. Many men are showing up and working with no plan, no aim, no mission.

A recent article in the New Yorker claims that men are falling behind. Aside from the academic struggle, cases of overdrinking, overdosing, as well as suicide are becoming more and more male dominated.[11] While the causes of this are complex, it can be boiled down to lack of vision. As men lack vision, they and the world around them suffer.

Hellen Keller, a blind and deaf woman, was once asked, "What would be worse than being born blind?" She replied, "The only thing worse than being blind is to have sight without vision." This epidemic is real.

Vision Is Rewarded

Our habits, whether good or bad, are driven by reward. Think about it, every habit you have comes with a "reward." A drinking habit gives a buzz, a masturbation habit gives a release, a workout habit gives feeling of accomplishment. Every habit gives reward.

Recent studies are showing social media addiction is linked to a release of dopamine. That red notification symbol on socials gives us a small dose of dopamine to the brain drawing the user to return later on for another fix. Every habit gives reward.

It can work against us, but it can also work for us.

Psychological research has found that when a man casts vision (for himself, family and work), there's a release of dopamine. Having and casting vision is a dopamine trigger!

It's no secret that today's males crave pleasure, hopelessly searching for satisfaction and seriously lacking motivation. Psychology is finding that simply living with vision accomplishes all three. Dopamine from vision casting provides pleasure, satisfaction and motivation to the male brain.

Whether you're an Evolutionist or Creationist, "Y" chromosome carriers were designed (or evolved) to cast vision. Psychologist Emily Deans writes, "The dopamine systems on the left side of the brain become more active with thinking and planning that is more long term."[12] Man is rewarded greatly for having and casting vision.

Where are you going to get your dopamine from? A phone notification, or foresight for your life, your home, and your team?

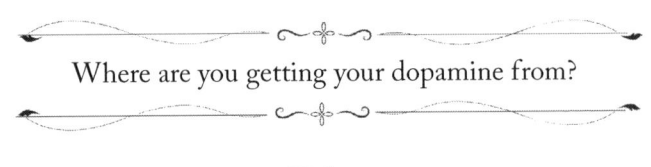

Where are you getting your dopamine from?

Unity

I played basketball in high school. I wish I had been better. Maybe if I'd been good enough, I wouldn't be self-publishing books...

Regardless, in high school I had an away game at a much larger school than mine (my high school at the time was less than 35 students, so everyone else was bigger).

After warmups, the refs blew their whistle to signal tipoff. At this point, the opposing coach sat down on the bench next to his players and opened a newspaper. He read that newspaper every minute of the game. I don't know why. It wasn't that he gave up on his team—his team was far more talented than us.

They were bigger than us. They should've mopped the floor with our little hick school, but we slaughtered them. They had no plays, no game plan, no vision. The team was disorganized as all get out, and as the score was run up on them, they turned on each other. Their "L" was completely on their coach.

This sad picture is the picture of many homes.

The wife, strong willed or not, is deep down looking for a worthy vision from her husband since he was designed to cast vision. However, the husband feels more respect and admiration at work so he gives his all at the office (as he should), but since the home is harder to lead— he grabs a newspaper (or his phone) sits back and leans into his wife to do what he should. This only frustrates the wife and the kids. As the home culture begins to decline, everyone turns on each other and we end up with the divorce rate our society suffers with.

Vision brings unity.

As Proverbs says, "Where there is no vision, the people suffer." A team with no vision falls apart. A company with no vision yields interdepartmental wars. Far and away more precious than any company, a family with no vision yields broken relationships. Vision always brings unity. It is upon the man to provide a clear and worthy vision. A man without vision for his roof is simply a boy adding to the tragic breakdown of the family.

The [Man]ual 43

Like it or not, the traditional family today has a massive target on its back. Only families with vision will survive. No more coaches reading the newspaper.

Clarity

My Junior year in high school I transferred from my one room school house to a local public school. My new high school was Division 1 athletics, and somehow I made the varsity basketball team. The day after tryouts I felt like I made an NBA team. Not only did I receive a jersey, I was given warm ups and team gear, something I'd never had nor dreamt of wearing.

Our first game was an away game. Mid-afternoon, I was excused from classes and was loaded on a bus in the athletic building parking lot. As I approached the bus, I noticed all my teammates were wearing the exact same thing— black windbreaker pants with a black windbreaker coat, all embroidered with our team name. They all looked like a scene from Squid Games. I, however, wore my typical white t-shirt and jeans. I left my windbreaker suit at home, I figured we're not in the Olympics and weren't required to look like we were attending opening ceremonies.

As I boarded the bus, my coach fiercely chewed me out. "We're going to look like we picked up a homeless hitchhiker on the way. You're not playing tonight, you're not team minded."

Team minded? What a bogus statement, my goal was to lead the team in assists.

I spent that evening fuming on the bench. I didn't understand the situation in the least. I came to believe my coach was mad simply because he wanted to look good.

The next week I was pulled into coach's office and he explained his vision. He said, "Junior, I want us to feel like a team long before the game starts. We're not just a unified team on the court, we're a team as we ride the bus. We're a team as we walk into the opposing gym. When you showed up looking like a dirty hitch hiker, we lost that vibe on our first game."

Regardless of whether I agreed with my coach's approach or not, his vision made sense. His anger made sense. His discipline made sense. Without his vision, I would've fought and struggled with my coach for the whole season.

Vision gives clarity to discipline.

This truth certainly isn't reserved for sports only. This reality is playing out behind the scenes in businesses, organizations and most importantly homes. Many kids live frustrated lives because they have no vision, therefore any discipline of them makes little to no sense. When disciplined, most kids usually think, "I'm being disciplined because I annoyed mom or dad or made them look bad." That's toxic and only breeds a future break in the relationship.

When a home has clear casted vision, discipline grows a child's heart and mind rather than driving a wedge.

Confidence

As I write this I'm sitting in a tiny farming community in the nation's dairy land— Wisconsin. I love it out here in the open spaces, bike trails, artisan bakeries, and generational run hardware stores. Farmers and their neighbors are salt of the earth people.

I recently learned something new about these farmers around here (well, their grandparents). One hundred years ago, the winter months could prove quite dangerous. Farmers aren't afforded a snow day, even in blizzard conditions they must care for their livestock. This led to many farmers losing their lives.

Believe it or not, in white out conditions, farmers would lose their bearings between their barn and their house. Walking one degree off course, they'd miss their house and end up in one of their fields. As the freezing wind and snow pelted them, they'd freeze to death. Wildly enough, this wasn't extremely uncommon. Many farmers died frozen, lost on their own property.

As such, farmer families feared blizzards. So they did something simple yet ingenious. They tied a rope from their house to their barn (like a cave explorer). This rope would then keep them on track when the winds whipped up and visibility changed. A simple rope saved many lives. The rope not only guided, it gave farmers confidence as they went about their work during storms.

This is vision.

Vision doesn't just guide our lives to making an impact, it gives confidence that we have something to hold onto and go after even in the midst of life's confusing storms.

The world will change. Culture will ebb and flow. Passions will shift. Friends will come and go. News outlets sell a buffet of different fears each day. Vision is a constant. Life has storms, and storms take the lives of people struggling to see. Vision is the guiding rope.

Regardless of the changing world and shifting culture, what are you going after? What are you producing under your roof? What mark are you aiming to leave? That doesn't change.

Men provide vision. Men provide the constant. Men tie the rope, cast the vision, and remind the roof where the rope is. It gives unity, clarity and confidence. A man without vision will lose himself (and others) on his own property. A man without vision is toxic. A man without vision just simply isn't a man.

Junior Ziegler

Chapter Challenge

Spend some time reflecting on the vision of your life. How do you want to be remembered? What words do you want associated with your life?

Write down your personal life vision.

If you have a family, do the same with and for your family.

THE {MAN}UAL

Junior Ziegler

Chapter Five

THERMOSTATS & THERMOMETERS

Venice, Italy, 1592. At the age of 28, Galileo settles into his new home a few blocks from St. Anthony Basilica.[13] The local university recently poached the increasingly popular Galileo with a pay increase— three times what he was making in Florence.[14] How could he turn down such an offer? With a drastic increase in income, Galileo was able to afford not only his artistic cravings, but also his scientific research ventures.

One such venture was his curiosity about heat. Galileo wasn't the first to take an interest in measuring heat. Ancient philosophers and early scientists had studied the variation between the freezing point of water and the boiling point of wa-

The [Man]ual 51

ter, but the large gap between freezing and boiling temperatures had remained untested. The mystery remained. One day Galileo desired an extra layer of clothing and the very next day he was sweating. How can this difference in heat around him be measured?

His curiosity led him to create something many elementary kids see in their science rooms— the "thermoscope". By trapping air in a glass tube and placing in a container of water or wine, Galileo found the air would expand and contract depending on heat around it.

20 years later, Galileo's colleague added a scale to the "Thermoscope" giving us the beginnings of the "thermometer"— a tool that measures heat by reacting to the temperature around it.

Thermometers react to temperature. Thermostats set the temperature.

Many men are thermometers of their home, reacting to the temperature, instead of thermostats, setting the temperature of their home.

Home Temperature

Dads don't like you touching their thermostats, it's the basis for many old jokes. He sets the house temperature because he pays the bill. Yet all too often, men so easily forget they set the temperature vibe of the home. When this happens, they resort to simply being a thermometer reacting to those in the home instead of setting a healthy culture.

I learned this the hard way.

Covid was rough in my home. Not because my wife and I disagreed on how to handle it. It was rough because, at the time Covid hit, my family was between houses. To save a little more for a downpayment on a new place, we opted to live in my parent's basement for "up to 2 months." It was fun for the first couple of weeks, like a big family campout.

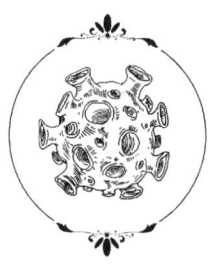

When covid hit, perfectly safe outside playgrounds and nature parks were shut down and families were forced to hunker down. So there my wife and I were with 3 kids in a tiny basement. Nowhere to go. No matter how much you love someone, living in close quarters like that while trying to get work done is at best frustrating. Not to mention, it's pretty hard having sex in your parents basement when your 3 kids are in a bed 5 feet away. So the valuable husband / wife connection wasn't strong.

On top of that, for an outdoorsy family to be cooped up in a basement, intimacy challenges, stress of trying to work in the same room kids are running around. It began to wear hard and fast.

One morning I was trying to help my oldest, who was in first grade at the time, sign on to her "virtual school." The software wasn't working correctly, my daughter was getting worried about missing class (nerd), and my younger two were fighting over something ridiculous. With my parents within earshot, I lost my cool. All the frustration boiled over like a mento in a diet coke. I took a tone I shouldn't have and reprimanded my daughter for something she couldn't help.

It was an embarrassing moment. When the pressure was on, I took the form of a thermometer reacting to everything around me.

The [Man]ual

Come to think of it, almost all of my husband and dad fails have come from me acting as a thermometer adopting the tones and frustrations around me instead of acting as thermostat and setting a new, healthier temperature.

After being an idiot and reprimanding my daughter for her faulty virtual school software, my dad (who never steps on my toes) simply said, "A constantly frustrated leader won't pass their values on to their kids." Dang it. I'll never forget that moment. I had to change from a thermometer to a thermostat if I wanted a chance at having a good relationship with my kids when they're older.

In our family, the first half of Covid was miserable. After that, we made some needed changes making the second half of covid extremely memorable. We had so much fun together, packing up my truck and driving to states with open parks. The second half had moments we'll always look back on.

The tense culture was on me, I had to change the temperature. The culture under a roof is provided by the man. The roof comes to ruin when he acts like a thermometer.

The most toxic homes I've witnessed have been homes where the dad didn't set the culture but reacts to people and situations in the home. Men don't adopt the emotions of situations, they lead their roof and teams to healthier cultures.

The Tone Temperature

I'm a terrible counselor. I tried to minor in counseling in college and I was kicked out of the program, not because of grades but because of my "lack of empathy." Whatever. I'm getting better…I think…

Regardless of my gifting, my wife and I periodically do pre-marriage counseling with young couples before their big day. My wife is far better at this than I am. Often our conversations will lead to tones. Many small fights between couples and families start and are exacerbated by unhealthy tones. It's on the man to confront unhealthy tones and set a new one. But it's far easier said than done.

Here's what often happens…

A saint of a mom is home with her kids who are running her ragged all day. The kids fight over the dumbest of arguments and she's on referee duty. On top of that, every 5 minutes the little monsters demand attention and help from her. She's a ref, a cook, a maid, and a house cleaner and it's far less thankful than the career she had. By the end of the day, she's mentally exhausted and thoroughly discouraged. She's an MMA cage fighter constantly in the final round trying to avoid her own K.O.

It's then the husband walks in the door after work. He's had a day of frustrating meetings and deals that fell through. In a way, he's hoping to come home to a house that is happy to see him. When he steps in, he finds his wife on her last nerve. It feels like he didn't step into his home, but rather a smoldering war zone.

Though she doesn't intend or even notice, her tone matches her exhaustion. After the 73rd fight, her wick is depleted and the tone is sharp with the kids as well as her husband.

It's at this very moment the man is tempted to help his girl by adopting her frustration. Like a WWE tag team, he comes in with a smackdown hoping to do what men love to do, solve the problem, therefore, winning the affection he wants from his wife.

The [Man]ual   55

When this doesn't work, the frustration grows and spirals. Now the husband and wife are talking to each other with sharp tones and the culture of the home is at a new low.

However, when we rewind this whole situation we find the issue at the beginning. The man walked through the front door as a thermometer. The intentions may have been right, if he can take the frustration of his girl maybe she'll feel a weight lifted. But what she needed in that moment was a thermostat. She needed a fresh partner to walk in, give her a break to let her breathe, and lead the kids to a healthier place. The gap between coming home and dinner is a pivotal moment for young dads to lead the home to a better place before dinner.

While this illustration is for young dads, this situation plays itself out in many different ways in every stage of life. This happens constantly, not just in the home with spouses but in the offices with teams and bosses. Good men set the temperature not react to it. They are constantly leading others to healthier places.

In the words of my dad, you can't pass your values on to those under your care if you're living in frustration.

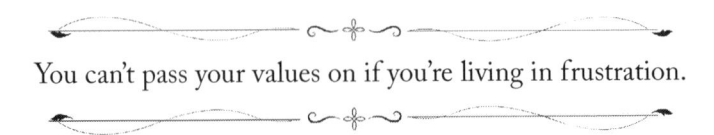

You can't pass your values on if you're living in frustration.

Thermometers don't influence. Your people need you to be a thermostat.

Thermostat Cheat Codes

I loved video games growing up. My family could never afford the nice systems, so while my friends had PlayStation 2's, I had the Sega Genesis. In middle school, I finally got a PlayStation 1. It was an exciting day, turning it on for the first time and hearing that Sony PlayStation start-up had me feeling like a President for the first time on Air Force 1.

After a few months of having a PlayStation, my friend Jake came over and blew my mind with something called "Cheat Codes". Apparently, if you pressed the controller buttons in a specific sequence you could unlock a demi-god status where you were invincible in the game. I had no problem cheating against a computer, it felt amazing to win with far less effort.

Life certainly doesn't come with cheat codes. But sometimes you run into helps that feel like cheat codes. I hope this next bit feels like that for you. While many of these "cheat codes" will be illustrated for dads with homes, each can creatively be adapted to offices, teams, and friendships. I can't speak to your specific contexts, you'll have to adapt. But I do believe your game changer lies on the next couple of pages…

Here are a few cheat codes to get more comfortable as a thermostat. This list certainly isn't exhaustive; you probably have a lot more you could add. These are just a few that have drastically helped me.

- **Periodically set a slow pace.**

Culture is bent toward speeding you up. Corporations make bank off leading customers toward quick-decision, impulse purchases. Restaurants make more money in faster meals, quicker table turnovers lead to more wallets in the seats. Television programming has found that faster-moving sitcoms keep viewers longer (just watch old sitcoms, they move slower). Everything around us speeds up the pace.

Not all of it is bad. A fast pace is good, run hard and fast. Sometimes the thermostat has to push for a fast pace, productivity is necessary.

However, all of it leads to homes being accustomed to a fast pace. When a home, team, or office only ever sprints, it breeds chaos. Chaos breeds frustration.

Life isn't one long sprint. Life also isn't a marathon. Life is a series of sprints. Humans were designed to push hard and then rest. The ebb and flow of fast pace to slow pace is healthy.

For many, the first act as a thermostat is learning when to slow things down.

Earlier this year, my wife mentioned to me that our home had become more complicated. We have three daughters, each of whom has a different sport. We're committed to church and serving. We also love being close to family and friends and entertaining. I had picked up a few international trips for speaking engagements. All of it was filling our shared calendar.

I wasn't setting a healthy pace.

A mom once admitted to me that she would feel anxiety over empty space in the family calendar. Her family had become a family of sprinters.

Many families live frustrated because they live in a state of chaos. One event to another. It's up to the thermostat to set a healthy pace.

Bring on boredom. There's beauty in boredom. Most memorable moments as families are born out of times of boredom. Studies show that boredom encourages deeper thinking and creativity. [15]

Periodically and intentionally set the temperature to boredom. You'll get pushback in those moments, but many of those times will birth beauty.

- **Make the table mandatory.**

The dinner table is the most valuable piece of furniture in the home. It's a place that does more than hold food. The dinner table is a place where the family collides, days are reviewed, problems are solved, and voices are heard. The home is most often led from the dinner table.

Recent research has found that kids who eat at the dinner table with their family are 40% more likely to earn A's & B's in school.[16] Think about that, if your child was struggling with grades and a potential tutor promised 40% growth, you'd hire that tutor. The dinner table does that.

Make the dinner table (or conference table for staff) mandatory. No more triaging life and scarfing down dinner at the drive-thru or kitchen counter. Lead from the table.

The [Man]ual

Set a fun temperature.

One of the greatest ways to pass your values on is through fun and laughter, something that is tragically absent in many homes. Nobody will accept your influence if you don't have fun. Deep down, we want to be like people who are fun and enjoy life. Set a fun temperature.

Years ago an old study was conducted on coworkers who couldn't get along. Like many offices (and homes), these coworkers could hardly speak to each other and felt more comfortable bickering than working as a team. These participants were brought into a room to watch a comedian. At first, the tension was felt and the laughs were few. After several minutes the laughter began to build and by the end, the enemy coworkers were laughing together. They left the room laughing and joking with each other.

There is something about laughing. It's the first emotion we feel comfortable displaying. Beyond that, laughing deepens connections. This is one of the reasons Jesus loved joking. People liked being around Him, despite what old cathedrals make it look like—Jesus was actually fun.

A good thermostat will set a fun temperature.

This takes creativity, but it's worth it. Go adventure. Learn the interest of those under your care and find ways to indulge in those interests together. Try the hobbies of those under your care, and laugh at yourself when you're not as good at it as they are. You will gain relational equity by entering their world and having fun.

One of my daughters loves gymnastics, I'm as flexible as a toothpick. When she's had a rough day at school, I'll head outside with her and try a cart-wheel…just to get us laughing.

I look like an idiot, and I hurt for 3 days—but it's worth the smiles. The relational equity is a good bonus too.

In the words of The Joker, "Why so serious?" Go have some fun, and lead with some periodic laughter. Nobody is actually influenced by a stoic, frustrated leader—that's toxic.

- **Three spoonfuls of sugar for every spoonful of medicine.**

In the words of my childhood crush Mary Poppins, "A spoonful of sugar makes the medicine go down."

Some people are only medicine people, and quite frankly they're a drag to be around. Medicine people feel big and useful by diagnosing people's problems and prescribing solutions. They are always correcting and nobody wants to be around them. I feel for those who are stuck in a home with them.

Other people are only sugar people, and quite frankly they're often annoying after a while. They usually have the best of intentions, make people feel great (or sometimes make people like them). They're just a bunch of smoke blowers.

Find a good ratio. The best thermostats have an average of three encouragements for every one correction.

You must still correct. The hardest part of leading is having hard conversations in grace, but that's foundational leadership. You can't lead if you can't have a hard conversation with love. However, those dreaded conversations go far better and are less awkward if there's been sugar before and after.

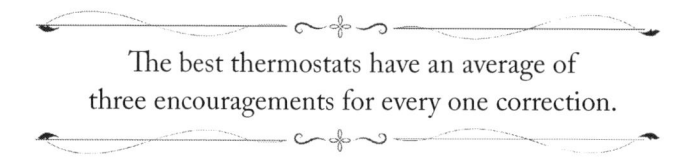

> The best thermostats have an average of
> three encouragements for every one correction.

The [Man]ual

Get to church.

Ok, maybe you're not into the church scene—props to you for reading a book from a pastor. But hear me out.

Multiple studies have shown that families that attend church tend to be healthier and closer. It's certainly not a given, I know a lot of church families whose kids don't want to return. Usually, those kids saw different parents under the roof than in church. Statistically, the church is a huge help.

Men, far be it for the wife to drag the family to church. That's on you. And if you call yourself a Christian, you have no excuse. The family should never wake up and think, "Are we going to church today?" It should be a given, and that is led by dad.

The Fastest Route To Being A Thermostat

I have a podcast with one of my best friends called, "Two Dudes In A Canoe". You should listen to it (unless you hate this book then don't because you have no taste ☺). My co-host has a life rule that I've adopted as my own. His life rule is "Fill the Keurig."

We have a Keurig Coffee Maker in our office, and it's annoyingly dry most of the time. It's frustrating because a sink is within two feet of the coffee maker, but for some reason, most people hit a button and just zone out as their brew sprinkles out. My friend made it his rule every morning, the first thing he does as he enters the office is fill the Keurig for everyone whether he's getting coffee or not. It's a simple act of service that reminds him that his day as a leader will be serving everyone around him. It's this philosophy that has made him one of the greatest thermostats I know.

The fastest route to being a thermostat is serving those in your care. In my opinion, the greatest "thermostat" to ever walk this earth was Jesus Christ. Everything changed after His life. He literally split how we measure history. He came to serve.

Passionately be that.

Thermostats dream of ways to set their partner up for a successful day. How can you make your coworker's day more successful? How can you clear a path so that your spouse has a better day because it started and ended with you?

Serve them by being the person who has the conversation everyone is avoiding. Serve them by walking toward what everyone else walks away from. Serve them by making things fun and enjoyable. Serve them by leading strong and providing security.

One of my life goals is that I want my wife to look forward to my arrival. I want my presence to make a noticeable difference to her. I want her to feel that when I'm around she's more successful.

To accomplish this, I have a few personal rules before leaving the house in the morning. Before I walk out the door, I must have the dishwasher emptied and reloaded. Just a little act to help her day. It's not her job anyway, but having it finished just makes for an easier morning.

I won't leave without the kids being fed, just one less thing for her to think about. I have to make the bed. She's never asked me to do these things and often tells me she'll get it. But for all of my mess ups and shortfalls, these little acts set a healthier temperature.

Thermostats serve. They look to set everyone else up for success because when everyone is succeeding, the temperature is nice.

I firmly believe that when a true man's head hits the pillow every night, he's thoroughly exhausted. He served his peers and reports in the office, and then he drove home and served his roof.

The quickest route to being a thermostat is serving. Thermometers are toxic, but thermostats change the world.

Chapter Challenge

Where & how have you been acting as a thermometer and not a thermostat?

What changes need to be made for you to become more of a thermostat?

How will you make those changes?

Chapter Six

Home Protection

Legend tells of a beautiful, old American Indian tradition. A major part of the man's provision was to bring up his son in bravery to be a dependable protector of the tribe. Even as a child, a young boy would follow his dad to learn the art of hunting, fishing, as well as scouting. By the time a boy reached 13, he knew his land, his traditions, and the way of survival— but there was one more test

On the night of a boy's thirteenth birthday, he was placed in a remote forest to spend a night alone in the wild. Until this point, a boy had never been outside the protection of the tribe

or the security of his family. Yet there he sits alone in a thick forest miles away, blindfolded with the sun setting.

After a period of time, the boy was allowed to remove his blindfold. The dark night sky was covered by tree tops providing no light to see. Every twig snap would send his imagination running wild of beasts lurking in the darkness around him ready to pounce. All night long, the boy sat anxiously alert waiting for the sun to rise and illuminate his surroundings.

After a sleepless night of terror, the morning glow of the sun would begin to illuminate the thick forest around him. This is when the boy's eyes would start to pick up on the outline of a path.

It's around this moment, the boy would experience a shocking realization that he would not soon forget. For standing just a few yards from him stood a man...his father...armed with bow and arrow. Dad had been there all night long.

The night wasn't just a night for growing bravery in the young boy, it was also a night the boy learned what it was to be a man. To be present in difficulty and quietly protect. Good men create challenging yet safe environments.

> Good men create challenging yet safe environments.

This idea doesn't just come from an old American Indian tradition, this is a major characteristic of the God of the Bible. Whether you believe in Him or not, just go with me for a second...

This life is drenched in challenge and struggle. Christian or not, you've tasted this—maybe even deeply. When somebody decides to live for God, this doesn't change (if anything it invites more pressure and tension). Christians call this "sanctification" which is just a big word for God working on a person to make them more like Jesus. This process is hard. God will call people to take risk, to sacrifice, to humble themselves. To "follow Jesus" is to accept challenge.

God creates challenging environments—it's all through Scripture. God has 100+ year-old Abraham climb a mountain. He asks 80+ year-old Moses to climb mountains and lead a nation of vulnerable, former slaves through a desert. He leads little red-headed David to duel with a war-seasoned giant. God is constantly leading people into challenge.

Yet, at the same time, one of the most repeated commands in Scripture is, "Fear not." On top of that, Scripture is littered with the idea of God being a refuge, God going before His own, God protecting.

This creates a curious yet beautiful tension. There's challenge, yet safety to fall back on. There's great power in both challenge and safety, something men are to create.

Here's where this can get tricky. One without the other leads to toxicity. Challenge without safety causes pain and brokenness. Challenge without safety at best flirts with abuse. A man who challenges without creating a safe environment is a brute of a man, the classic "toxic masculinity" if you will.

On the flip side, safety without challenge leads to soft, unproductive people who never reach their potential. People don't grow in this environment. Safety without challenge has led to the difficulty our society faces right now—snowflakes addicted to comfort with no ability to problem-solve or sweat. A man who creates a safe roof with no challenge is a man who never boots the baby birds out of the nest. This is a helicopter father. It's a boss who never has a hard conversation to push his crew to new heights. Though this is often seen as the "kind" or maybe "passive" man—he's still toxic because he wastes people's potential.

Much of the power of a man lies in his ability to create challenging, yet safe environments.

The Roller Coaster Bar

Adrenaline Junkies will disagree, but the truth is we were designed to desire safety. Even adrenaline junkies (at least the ones who live) still have a mind to check safety measures before cliff jumping.

Next time you go to a theme park, watch for this. After people stand in line for 2 hours and they finally sit down on the rollercoaster, the bar will come over them. What will a lot of people do at that moment? They shake the bar. Why? They're testing their safety. Has it locked? Is it broken? Let's give the bar a good shake test.

I use this illustration at a camp when I train our camp counselors. This is exactly what kids do when they get to camp. During the first few days at camp, they shake the safety bar. Many campers (at least I did) want to test the limits of their camp counsellor. Will the counselor enforce the rules? And though they think they want a free-spirited leader who lets them get away with anything, the truth is they feel safe when the bar doesn't shake and the leader leads strong and gracious.

In the 1960's an old study was done on school fences. Most schools had fences around the schoolyard. The students could run freely at recess within the safety of the fences. The fences were taken down and something interesting happened. Researchers observed the kids played much closer to the school building. The fences had provided a safety that led kids to play more freely.

It's sometimes subconscious, but it is human nature to desire safety.

This is the role of men in society. Good men provide safe environments for the people in their care to grow.

A few ways to balance safety and challenge…

Set Clear Expectations

This is why Chapter 4 is so vital. Clear expectations flowing from vision provide safety. People don't feel safe in nebulous conditions. Offices and homes that feel safe have clearly outlined expectations.

This goes against today's grain. It's a common thought (a thought I still personally fight) that it's gracious to be a free-spirited leader. I'm a free spirit at heart. I like to think that allowing there to be a lot of "gray areas" is gracious. Despite what many of my fellow millennials champion, gray isn't gracious. Families and organizations that allow a lot of "gray" don't produce healthy products nor facilitate clear safe places to grow.

Going back to the God of the Bible, God isn't a God of much gray. Sure, there's some gray in the Bible, but for the most part, the Bible is clear and pretty black and white. Don't get me wrong, the God of the Bible is overly gracious, you can't get more gracious than taking on skin to die in our place. He's gracious, but He's also clear and gives His people black-and-white expectations.

Clarity is kindness.

I try to remember "clarity is kindness" anytime I need to have a hard conversation or I'm training someone. Though it might feel like it, being wishy-washy and gray simply isn't kind—nor does it reflect the leadership of God.

Be clear. In a world of chaos and double standards, kids need clarity. Your home should be one of the most safe environments for families to enjoy and grow because there's clarity in expectations.

My worst class in college started out as my favorite. It was my freshman year at Madison College in Madison, WI. I love Madison, I named my oldest daughter Madison. The city has beautiful eccentricities. It's a city where traditional farmers and old hippies often collide. In one of my first classes of college, a man resembling the great Willie Nelson walked in. He handed out a loose syllabus that looked as though it were typed in a cloud of special smoke. I immediately figured this semester was going to be great. This old hippie is going to be cool with whatever. I can phone this one in. This guy is the best!

I ended up spending that class anxiously trying to figure out a man who hadn't figured himself out yet. Forget his free-spirited approach to assignments, his unclear expectations led to a lot of frustration in trying to figure out what he was looking for. To be candid, I don't remember what that class was even about and it wasn't because there was a second-hand Snoop like haze in the room. His lack of clarity in the name of being the nice guy only led to irritation from both the teacher and the students.

This story is playing out in many homes and offices. In an attempt to be gracious and "nice," men can facilitate environments where expectations aren't spelled out. This then frustrates families and teams as they underperform trying to figure out what's expected instead of accomplishing what's expected. There is no safety in lack of clarity. Nor is there even the slightest amount of healthy challenge.

Clear expectations are kind. They lead to safety and challenge.

Have Open Communication

Before you skip this, we're not talking about appeasing your girl's wish that you'd talk more about your feelings. I don't want to touch that.

One of the staff values on the team I work is "Inspect not expect." Expectations are necessary. They need to be clear—but they can't just be expected. Your team, your kids, and your staff won't do what you expect, they'll do what you inspect.

Environments that have challenge have inspection. Nobody is challenged when there is no accountability for the work they do.

In the same way, nobody feels safe on a team or family where there's no inspection. This might feel backward, because we hate the feeling of our work being inspected. I mean construction crews don't necessarily feel safe with OSHA lurking on the premises. But I'd bet you the next crew coming in will feel safer knowing the floor they work on was inspected. I feel safe when I board a plane that's been inspected.

Inspection of expectations creates safe environments. A man who doesn't run from confrontation creates a safe roof. Often, I find men lack this open communication because they don't want to look like they micromanage.

Aside from the fact that many of the tech and business giants were micromanagers (like Thomas Edison and Walt Disney), open communication with your family and team isn't micromanaging. The truth is, confrontation is necessary to keep expectations clear.

Expectations are worthless without open communication.

Sometimes we lack open communication because don't want to "micromanage," but more often than not **we lack open communication because it's just hard**.

In the summer of 2010, I was 23. A lot happened that summer. I graduated college, I got married and I took over the student ministry at the church I'm still at. Maybe I had the potential to lead, but I was a bad leader.

The team I took over wasn't healthy. Two very influential, seasoned leaders on the team didn't want me as their leader (I guess I can't blame them). They communicated their disapproval of me in many words to other leaders and even a few students. Instead of grabbing the bull by the horns, I decided I was going to just outlast them—gain credibility with others and replace the bad apples, which I eventually did. But I wish I could do it over. I made a big, yet common mistake.

Because I didn't trust them, and because they were constantly bucking my leadership—I communicated minimally with them. I led in a cowardly fashion. Oh, I could paint myself as a saint and tell you I just didn't want to fight and was trying to be gracious, but the real truth is I was lazy and lacked courage.

Maybe it's understandable to you, but for me, it's not. And it's not because I'm being hard on myself. I call myself a follower of Jesus and God doesn't treat me that way. I buck His leadership, I can be difficult to deal with and God doesn't lead me in a cowardly way. He convicts me. He uses people around me to challenge me. God has open communication with me.

Maybe you're of a different belief, and that's fine. We can at least agree that where there's a lack of communication, people don't feel safe. Women don't feel safe in a marriage where communication sucks. Children look for safety outside of the home where communication is unhealthy. You can tell a child's confidence in the safety of their home simply by how much and what they can go to their dad about.

Communication is a major metric of any relationship. Open communication through inspection and listening leads to challenge and safety.

Have More Fun

I know, we talked about this in Chapter 5 so I won't beat a dead horse. It also can't be left unsaid, fun environments feel safe. Case in point, I've never felt safe at the DMV. Seriously, the DMV might be staffed with officers who look like they handled 36 street fights on their former assignment—but I don't feel safe. I'm dealing with grumpy Gretchen who's close to her pension. Her face looks like she started the 36 street fights the officers had to settle. She's raking me over the coals for asking where the bathroom is. As soon as I walk into the DMV, I feel on edge.

I feel the same in many homes. Fun cuts tension.

I once fielded a call in our church office. I usually don't because, again, I'm a terrible counselor. The call was from a mom who just caught her son doing something weird. I felt for her, the dad was a deadbeat and out of the picture. She was overwhelmed by this weird situation that she now needed to handle. She explained the details of the situation and couldn't get over her own horror. She then asked, "What should I do?"

I responded, "First go have some fun. Rent bikes and ride along the lake. Go go-karting. Go see a movie and get some ice cream."

She interrupted me and asked if anyone else was there to talk to.

I get her confusion in my response, but there was a reason for it. She needed to cut the tension. Things felt weird and confusing, therefore unsafe. Having some fun gives a shot of safety in moments that feel uneasy.

I know I'm repeating myself, but my goodness—men should lead the fun. We're not. If you're fun, it's just harder to be toxic.

Protect

Like the Indian Father quietly protecting his son as he struggles. It's God with us as He leads to challenge. Protection is a major part of manhood.

I realize it's the title of this chapter and we haven't really addressed the classic physical protection yet. Some guys will pick up this chapter, see the six shooters and think, "home protection," and get all amped, "Yea, let's talk guns and protecting the home." I'm not against that; I have several guns in my house. But I haven't really had to use them yet.

I know too many men with obsessively cleaned guns chomping at the bit to shoot an intruder like Barney Fife shooting from the hip. They love the idea of physically protecting the home, and that's great, but they constantly let other intruders in that kill the home.

Physical home protection is far easier than holistic home protection.

The second year of our marriage, my wife and I bought a small Spanish style stucco house. We renovated a lot of it. I loved that house, a lot of character. The day we bought that house, something in me switched. I suddenly felt more responsibility to protect. Before we were in a 3rd-floor apartment, hard to reach. Now we were in an actual house, this was the big time.

Soon after we bought our house, something embarrassing happened that my wife loves to remind me of. At 2 AM one night, I awoke to the sound of voices outside. At first, I thought I was dreaming, but the voices persisted. Seeing as how I'm the man, I got out of bed and patrolled the house, looking out the windows at a dark but empty yard.

I sat down in our living room and kept hearing voices. Am I going crazy? Then I heard my storm door open. I flipped the light on and the door closed. Someone is playing with my door.

At this point, I'm wide awake with adrenaline. Once again, the storm door opens and I see my doorknob begin to turn. It was at this moment I learned whether I was fight or flight—I'm fight. I ran at the door and punched through the window cutting my arm up good.

Apparently on the other side of the door were a couple of high schoolers from my church who were just pranking me. They got me good.

I felt this great pressure to physically protect my wife. That pressure became even greater when my wife gave me three little girls. My paranoia often has me up at night checking and rechecking the safety of our home.

But I wish I was just as passionate about protecting my house from the other intruders. You may wonder who they are. Here's a non-exhaustive list of intruders looking to infiltrate your home. By no means am I sounding the alarms and advising everyone to live in a bunker away from society. But knowing the enemy is more than half the battle. This list is far from exhaustive, you can add your own but here's a start…

You

During the War of 1812, U.S. Navy Master Commandant Oliver Perry said something that a cartoonist Pogo made popular, "We have met the enemy and he is us."[17] Sometimes the enemy is us. We have every intention of protecting our home or our team from an intruder who would abuse, meanwhile, our attitude, lack of love, distance, and words kill our homes and teams each day.

A good percentage of effective marriage counseling addresses a man's attitude. He kills the marriage with a lack of trying. He might jump at the sight of a turning doorknob at 2 AM, but slowly kills the home with passivity and attitude.

Is the intruder ever you?

·⚜· Culture

I'm not "anti-culturist" demonizing anything new and advocating we shelter children while they churn their own butter and don't understand how to turn on a TV. If that's you, that's fine—just don't raise too weird of a kid. Too much shelter often leads to rebellion. I'm not pushing over-sheltering kids.

However, look around—it's obvious there are agendas all around us. The school curriculum is rapidly changing, and proof is in the pudding- test scores in the United States are declining.[18] It would be ignorant to believe there is no target on the minds of children.

Men are to lead as filters. Men must care about what does and doesn't become normal in the mind of their children.

The Amish have a fascinating way of conducting their community. I'm not advocating we become Amish, but I do appreciate many of their values. Of course, the Amish are far differ-

The [Man]ual 79

ent than any other community in the United States, living very much like how people lived over 100 years ago. I used to think they chose a moment in history and decided not to adopt anything new after that moment, but that's not true.

When a new invention (such as a car, radio, or roller-skates) hits the market, many independent Amish communities will test the new invention within their community. A test group within the community will try out the product whether it be a car or bicycle. After a given time, they convene together to decide whether that product helped or hurt their community.

For example, the story goes that when the Amish tried the car they found that people within the community didn't visit their relatives on Sunday like everyone else. The car owners could now travel far in a short amount of time and so on Sabbath when everyone gathers as family, the car owners would leave town. They found the car hurt the community and they decided to not have cars. Now I like my truck and am keeping it, but their intentionality is something to take note of.

Men are filters. Men should know what their children are listening to and reading. Not to be a brute and ban anything that might be off, but at the very least have an open conversation about it and maybe consider together whether it should be limited or removed.

Culture as a whole isn't something to condemn, but it is something to filter. This is the job of men. We protect by filtering. And for Christians, we filter by using Scripture, not our opinions or preferences.

·❧· Idols

The word "idol" drums up images of ancient civilizations dressing up and dancing around golden statues. It's easy to believe idols simply aren't a potential threat to your home. They are.

Think of it this way, if you and I were to travel to a tribal land, if we were to walk into one of their huts or homes, and we found right in the center of their home a statue—we would think "Well that's obvious idolatry." Yet if you were to walk into my living room, I have all my furniture facing the same thing- my television hanging on the wall.

My guess is you've checked your phone at least once since reading this chapter. Sure, maybe it's because my writing gets a bit boring (I won't argue that), but I would add it's also because you probably can't go 30 minutes without looking at your phone. It captivates your attention and affection.

Idols are anything that consume too much of our attention and affection. It's sports. It's relationships. It's television. It's video game systems.

Men are to be protectors. Protectors of idols in the home. It starts with us modeling freedom from idols, and it continues with graciously confronting potential idols that invade our roof.

·⁒· Unresolved Conflict

This is where many extended families and friendships begin to crumble, bitterness grows in a home like dandelions in that organic neighbor's yard. It starts with an issue that was swept under the rug or not properly dealt with. This bitterness then begins to infect and deteriorate.

One of the hardest jobs of a man is to detect and properly yet graciously confront unhealthy tension in the relationships entrusted to his care. Unresolved conflict ultimately leads to loneliness in age.

Future fun family reunions are the goal. This intruder will kill that potential.

Safety Comes At A Cost

Everything has a price. A family that enjoys a healthy, safe environment isn't free. The man foots the bill. The good man makes himself uncomfortable so others can be comfortable

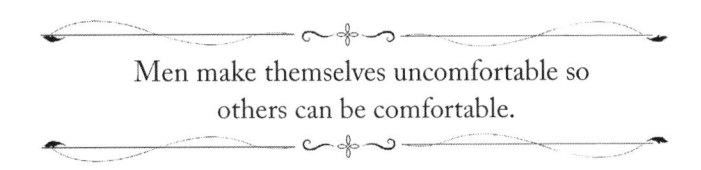

> Men make themselves uncomfortable so others can be comfortable.

The American Indian boy's father had it right. Men engage the scary situation. They are present. They quietly protect. They lead with clarity and open communication. They're fun to have around. They lead as filters, confronting idols, and resolving the conflict. This safety with challenge cause others to flourish.

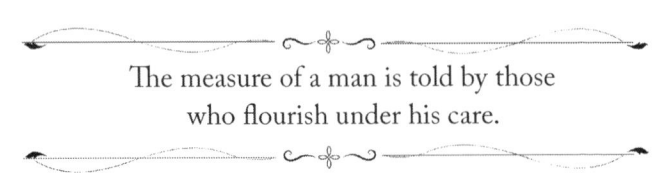

> The measure of a man is told by those who flourish under his care.

Chapter Challenge

Which enemy listed in this chapter has been invading your roof the most?

What are you going to do to provide better protection against that enemy?

Where do you need to become more uncomfortable?

THE {MAN}UAL

Chapter Seven

Deepen Your Roots

Not many know the name Clarence Jordan. Clarence is one of those many good men whose faithful sweat and sacrifice flew under the radar of pop culture. A well-educated man, Clarence held not one but two Ph.D.s, one in agriculture and the other in Greek & Hebrew. His mind, his abilities, and his education permitted him to do just about anything Clarence desired. Great fortune was easily within reach.

Source: **koinoniafarm.org**

Instead, Clarence decided to buy a farm in Americus, Georgia to give a place for poor whites and poor blacks to

The [Man]ual 85

come together and live and work. As a believer in God, Clarence dreamt of displaying God's beautiful diversity and unity on the same property. Today this is a beautiful picture to most, however, in the 1940s deep south, this was a death wish. Clarence quickly became a villain, receiving threats from neighbors, those in surrounding communities, and even those within his own church.

There were frequent boycotts to stop the sale of his farm's produce. When workers ran errands into town, they would return to their trucks with its tires slashed. For 14 years, many did all they could to make Clarence's life and business a living hell.

In 1954, Clarence's work of uniting blacks and whites caught the attention of the Ku Klux Klan. The KKK along with allied community members and neighbors banned together to set fire to Clarence's farm and home. As mob members with guns chased off black families (except for one family who refused to leave). Others set fire to Clarence's home and riddled it with bullets. The Georgia night sky glowed from the farm crops ablaze in fire.

As Clarence and his terrorized family ran through the mob, they could recognize voices under hoods, voices of their neighbors and fellow community members. One voice they recognized was a local well-known newspaper reporter.

The next morning, that same newspaper reporter returned to the smoldering farm to sink his teeth into the new juicy story he played a part in. He didn't find Clarence inside his bullet-hole perforated home. He was hoping to find Clarence packing his bags making for a great picture. But Clarence wasn't in the house. Instead, the reporter found Clarence out in the field planting.

"I heard the awful news," he said with a twinge of excitement in his voice. "...and I came out to do a story on the closing of your farm."

Clarence kept his hand to the dirt and remained silent. The reporter kept pushing and baiting Clarence into any sort of angry statement for readers to eat up, but Clarence kept planting. Finally, the reporter blurted out with a tone of frustration, "Well, Dr. Jordan, you got two of them Ph.D.s and you've but fourteen years into this farm and there's nothing left of it all. Just how successful do you think you've been?"

Finally, Clarence broke his focus on the soil and shot his penetrating blue eyes at the reporter and firmly said, "About as successful as the cross."

An awkward, yet effective pause allowed the comment to sink in deep.

Clarence continued, "Sir, I don't think you understand us. What we're about is not success but faithfulness. We're staying. Good day."[19]

Clarence's farm still stands to this day doing what it did 80+ years ago. His name might have flown under the radar, but his faithfulness has quietly impacted generations and the world around them.

His story begs the question— are you chasing success or faithfulness?

Don't get me wrong, the two aren't always mutually exclusive—but one always takes priority. Which do you have your sights set on?

I know too many guys who bounce around. Guys who are gifted leaders with more potential than I can even dream of having—but they can't stick with anything. They're always hopped up talking about something new. And nobody cares, because they've relegated themselves to the boy who cries wolf. Their "new venture that will explode with results," sounds awfully familiar to the last one that yielded nothing.

Are you chasing success or faithfulness? What if some of those shiny opportunities are just bait distracting you from the mundane diamond in a rough that God has for you to chip away at?

In a world of rapid job turnover—leveraging jobs to climb ladders, high divorce rates, and church hoppers; faithfulness is quite foreign. Faithfulness is so foreign that it is often misunderstood. We start here.

Where do you actually bring value?

A common misconception is that faithfulness is just sticking to things. Sure. But what if those things suck? Then we're just faithfully unproductive. We're faithfully wasting time. We're faithfully doing lame things. I'd rather not be faithful at losing...

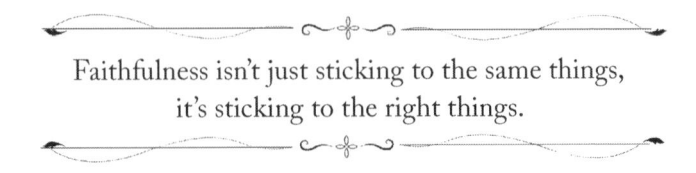

> Faithfulness isn't just sticking to the same things,
> it's sticking to the right things.

Here's what I mean. God designed you, and in a sense, His design is twofold. First, He designed you with a gift to be used in this life. The second part of His design is that He created a yearning in you to one day hear your Creator say, "Well done, my good and faithful servant." How you use your gift will determine hearing those words.

It's here a major problem presents itself: what's my gift? Most people don't necessarily ooze self-awareness. Case and point when you read the beginning of that sentence someone else came to mind ☺. It's hard to evaluate personal strengths and weaknesses. Sometimes we're too hard on ourselves, but more often than not we pick something we like and then decide on that to be our gifting merely because we enjoy it. Remember American Idol? The whole show was based on this human condition, thinking we're gifted where we're not. Most pastors I run into say they have the gift of "teaching." But I wonder if it's the "American Idol Syndrome."

Too many people neglect their actual gift because they convince themselves they're gifted elsewhere. They live a tragic life of unfaithfulness chasing something they weren't designed to thrive with.

Forgive me for ragging on one of the best movies of all-time —Rudy. I love the movie! It's a movie of determination and heart, a guy who sucks at football works his butt off to play a few plays for the Notre Dame Fighting Irish. It's heartwarming. But it's also tragic if you think about it. Rudy was convinced football was his thing. He threw himself fully at football...to play a few plays... What if Rudy would've thrown himself at his actual gifting? I venture to say, his determination and heart would've landed him with a far bigger accomplishment than playing a few plays for a college football team.

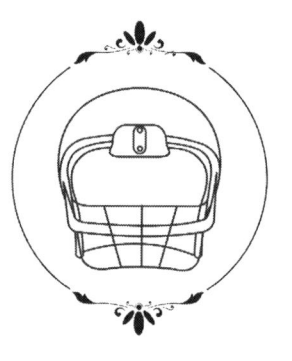

The [Man]ual

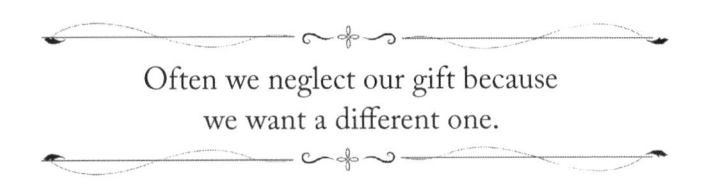

> Often we neglect our gift because
> we want a different one.

So how do we find our actual gifting?

I won't exhaust this idea as many books and personality tests have been developed to help people "identify their gifting." Often people flock to these tests to appease that little narcissism in all of us to learn more about ourselves. Maybe, I'm just jaded. I suppose there is value in some of that.

I like a more simplified approach. Want to find your gifting? Instead of embarking on an exciting journey of "self-discovery" to learn your hopes and dreams and inner child, how about just volunteering where you're most needed? Whether you like it or not, whether it aligns with your personality number or not, just do it. Go serve, go love people. Personal gifts have a way of surfacing in these environments.

Bottom line, to neglect your gift because you'd prefer a different one is to live unfaithfully.

Faithful men start self-aware. They accept their gifting (whether they'd choose it or not) and then they embark on a mission to craft it and utilize it in the mundane. Their craft blesses.

Rather than leveraging their craft to bring them attention (and then neglecting it when their gift doesn't serve them), men utilize their gift in the daily grind. Men who live faithfully power through their feelings and even lack of results simply to be faithful to their precious gift.

Someone Is Always Coming After You

Not to attack you, to replace you. Someone is always coming after you to fill your shoes.

What you do today, someone else will do tomorrow. Your title is temporary. Your office is just being held for the next person. You're simply just keeping your chair warm for the next guy. I don't mean to depress you, it's just a reality we must live with.

Will the next person be glad they took over for you?

You might know this from experience, but it's a privilege to take over for someone who has been faithful because they don't leave a mess. Faithful people always set up the next person for success, because they realize their life is about more than themselves. Their faithfulness outlives their lives. Their faithfulness benefits the next generation.

Have you ever noticed that faithful men aren't just faithful in the big things (like marriage). Rather it's many habits that mark everything they do. There is something about men who will finish well. It's like they have habits of "small" faithfulness, as though they are constantly living to set up the next person for success. It's Clarence Jordan inhaling smoke to plant the next batch of crops for his employees to harvest. It's George Washington Bush braving the Oregon Trail to send resources back for those who would come later. George was thinking of those coming after. It's the American Indian father standing by his son all night in order to hand success off to the next generation. The father was doing it for those coming after. Faithfulness isn't just large acts, **faithfulness is a life of small daily habits.**

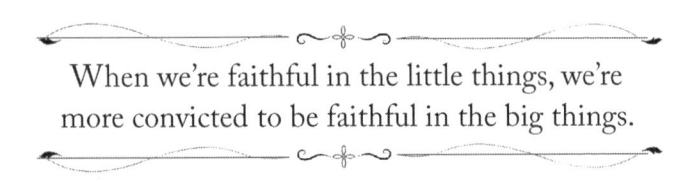

> When we're faithful in the little things, we're more convicted to be faithful in the big things.

Faithful Habits

Periodically young guys coming out of college will ask to meet with me about life, specifically their career path and hopes and dreams for the future. I love their teachability, they want to get started on the right foot. When they come into my office, I can tell they expect to talk about bigger topics like goal setting, leveraging opportunities, and boundaries—all of which are must-have conversations at some point I guess. However, I usually disappoint these guys with something far less flashy of a subject—little habits of faithfulness.

Here's how to start off on the right foot, build tiny habits of faithfulness. Make your bed. Mow your lawn. Shovel your driveway. Keep your car clean. Fill the Keurig. Aim to accomplish all the little things nobody claps for or posts about. When you're convicted by being faithful to all the little unseen things, you'll be positioned to take on the big more seen things.

I don't want a guy working for me who leaves his place with an unmade bed, walks past his unkept lawn, and gets into his sty of a car to come into work. He might be a nice guy, but I don't want him on my team—much less leading me!

Don't get me wrong, it's not about having a made bed or a clean car. Plenty of guys make their bed and drive to work in a clean car and then suck at their job and fail to lead their family. It's not about the made bed, it's about the way he leads his life. Does he aim to faithfully hit the small things that nobody pays attention to? If someone can't handle little with few eyes watching, he certainly won't handle much with many eyes watching.

We, especially in our younger years, tend to dream of success. There's nothing wrong with that. A man should have fire in his belly to be successful. I don't want my daughters marrying some schmuck with no dreams. If a guy doesn't have a vision and a pair of balls to chase that vision— I don't want him to marry my daughter. Desire for success is necessary.

However, dreaming of success without building little habits of faithfulness is toxic. A man who chases success more than faithfulness is a man who will never be able to handle true success.

Habits of faithfulness condition us to achieve and maintain success. Without the habits, a man has no real strength to steward and hold onto his success.

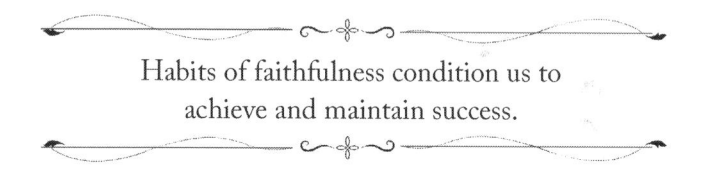

> Habits of faithfulness condition us to achieve and maintain success.

Plant Roots

As I write this, it's the hottest point of summer. This morning I was looking at my lawn trying to decide whether to cut it or leave it longer.

I decided to let my grass get longer, not because I've ditched my habit of lawn care but because I've heard the longer the grass—the deeper the roots. Since it's hot and dry, I want my grass to have deep roots to weather the heat and lack of water. The deeper the roots, the more healthy the lawn.

Our lives are the same. The deeper the roots, the healthier the roof. The deeper the roots, the greater the impact.

> The deeper your roots are, the greater your impact will be.

A lot of men are pushing through life with no real roots. They jump from one relationship to another, one city to another, one job to another. While there's nothing wrong with taking bigger opportunities, however, it can often come at the cost of deepening roots.

Deep roots are worth far more than our culture values it.

One of the reasons I've become less of a fan of professional basketball (this is just my opinion) is most players switch jerseys at the drop of a hat. Many professional basketball players are like kids dating in middle school, on to the next relationship as soon as something better comes along. It's one of the reasons we look up to guys who stick with their team and power through the dry spells.

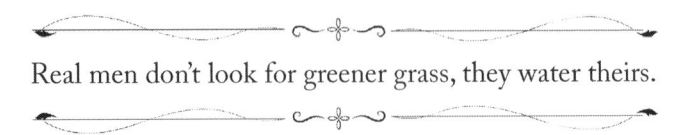

> Real men don't look for greener grass, they water theirs.

I wonder how different our world would be if men stopped hunting for the greener grass on the other side of the fence, and instead, we saw it as our job to plant roots and water ours.

All too often guys want to cash in on the faithfulness of another guy, and assume their green lawn, instead of planting roots to make their lawn healthy to hand it to the next guy. Men need to stop hunting and start farming. Stop hunting for the next big break and start farming your life into a big break.

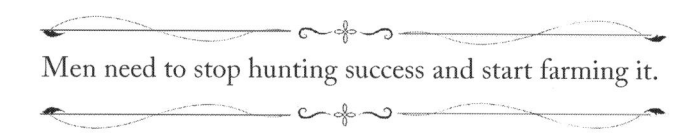

Men need to stop hunting success and start farming it.

Play The Long Game

I love instant gratification; it's one of my vices. I love low investment with quick return. Last year, I invested $5 in a cryptocurrency and two weeks later sold it for $150. I felt like Warren Buffet (until I lost my Covid handout in other cryptocurrencies…).

It's a rather addicting pursuit that most men are on. Low investment, quick return. It's what most of us tend to brag about. Buy a girl a drink, get laid. Flip a house on the cheap side, cash out. Create an app, sell it.

Not all low investment quick returns are wrong, but it often drives men to play the short game only. After all, the short-game money makers are exhilarating. However, when the dollar signs are taken out of the equation—there's not much of a legacy in a short game-only life.

The day the buzzer goes off and your clock has run out, it's the long game you'll be looking at. It's your marriage, your children, the deep-rooted relationships, the difference you made within the community.

We brag about the short-game money makers now, but one day we'll only talk about our long game. The worth of a man

The [Man]ual 95

isn't seen in his ability to flip a low investment into a big return. The worth of a man is seen in his ability to stick to what matters for the long haul.

Alexander Hamilton said that legacy is "...**planting seeds in a garden you never get to see.**" Faithfulness doesn't invite much praise. Faithfulness just isn't sexy in the moment. Not sure anyone has had flashes of beautiful faithfulness to admire in the moment. Faithfulness is always ahead of its time. The beauty of faithfulness is seen in the rear-view mirror.

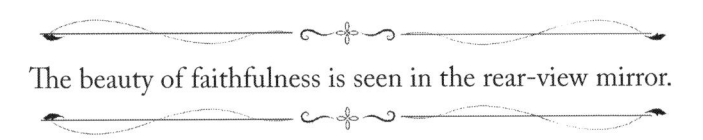

The beauty of faithfulness is seen in the rear-view mirror.

Final Thought: Be Mickey Not Rocky

In 1976, people flooded to the theaters to watch Sylvester Stallone's Rocky fight Spider Rico. Three years later those same crowds came back for Rocky II.

The box office success isn't as much owed to the sport of boxing as much as it is to the writing. Rocky is the protagonist the masses identify with. The struggle of man is relatable. Here's a no-name guy taking punches but keeps swinging for success. Rocky hit a nerve with the general public. We all feel Rocky's plight.

However, the real hero of the movie, in my opinion, is Mickey the trainer. To me, Mickey encapsulates what true manhood is. The unsung hero comes alongside the protagonist to give confidence and point toward success. Isn't this the basic role of man? To quietly be in the corner of those we care for, to train, to inspire, to walk through the difficulty with them, and take pleasure in their success?

Mickey is the hero.

It's here a major opportunity presents itself, but most miss it. Those around you see themselves as Rocky trying to fight through life to shine in success. They're taking their punches and dreaming of success. In a world full of Rockys, be Mickey. Who's Rocky without Mickey? Everyone needs a Mickey.

This is why the woman at the beginning of the book couldn't find good men. They exist. They're just in their people's corner, giving confidence and helping those in their care achieve success.

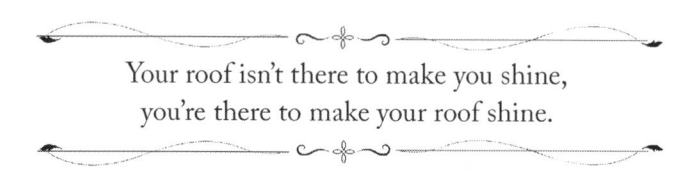

Your roof isn't there to make you shine,
you're there to make your roof shine.

Plant roots. Live faithfully. Play the long game. Be Mickey. Not only will your roof shine, you'll be living according to your design.

Chapter Challenge

What gift do you need to remain faithful to in crafting & using?

What "little faithful habits" do you need to incorporate into your week this week?

Who can you be a Mickey to?

Conclusion

Have Some Fire

I almost called the conclusion, "Don't Be Vanilla." But apparently "vanilla" most often refers to boring sex (which still applies—don't have boring sex). Knowing my luck, somehow a Karen with a blog would for some reason make it this far in the book, see the title and then get all bothered because she feels conviction over her vanilla sex life… As much as I love watching Karens lose it on dumb things, this isn't for her.

Too many guys are walking around as if they're neutered (and maybe they have been by their own Karen of a wife). But the reality is, they live internally frustrated with little fire in their belly to lead and push, they're just…vanilla… As such, they "create" boring homes, boring marriages, and boring teams… nobody's trying much of anything new. It's always the same old, same old.

The [Man]ual

A few months ago I was visiting a church with my wife. I try to make it a point to not be critical of the church when I go visit somewhere because it's lame. Pastors tend to be the biggest critics of other pastors and other churches, which only ever reveals just how insecure we are. The worst critics are pastors who failed in ministry.

Anyway, I'm visiting this church and enjoying another church community full of good people. There were a few weird moments, though, I noticed the word "hell" was removed from their music which I found interesting. Can't say hell in church? Jesus talked an awful lot about hell… Everything was toned down and neutered, nothing remotely edgy or exciting.

When the speaker got up, I could tell he was probably one of the nicest guys you'll ever meet. He looked like he stepped out of the "Leave It To Beaver" show. He was a clean-cut guy, as non-controversial as they come. He spoke with a gentle soft tone and rarely if ever showed any excitement.

Still holding onto my commitment to not be a critic, I was curious about what my wife thought. Mid-service, I leaned over to my wife and asked, "What kind of car do you think he drives?" Her reply almost had me interrupt the service with laughter. She replied, "Probably whatever his wife tells him to drive…"

Dang girl.

Don't get me wrong, I am not telling you to dress like Dog the Bounty Hunter tomorrow to prove you're not whipped by your wife. That's not my point. Most of my friends are clean-cut polo-sporting golfers and they're often more "manly" than me.

My point is, men were designed to push limits. Men were designed to shake things up. Men were designed to bring some excitement and spice things up. Men serve by pushing the envelope.

Too many men confuse "servant leadership" with being a coward.

Cowards don't push. Cowards live in vanilla. After all, you don't get critiqued if you're not doing anything. Many men lead in cowardly ways, trying to appease everyone—keep everyone happy. As such they frustrate most people around them. Servant leadership isn't giving everyone their way, that's being a coward.

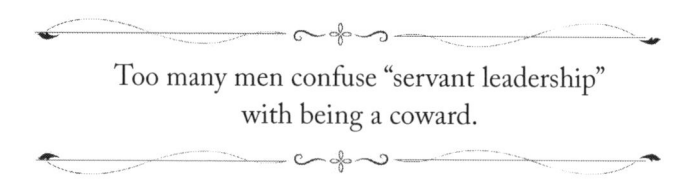

> Too many men confuse "servant leadership" with being a coward.

Servant leadership is ultimately leading for the benefit of those around them. Often what benefits others the most is challenge. The best leaders I have in my life challenge me, they push me. Those who just try to keep me happy aren't leading me.

We serve by making things less vanilla. We serve by shaking things up and making things uncomfortable. We serve by pushing hard enough that we get pushback. Because it's in that beautiful tension that we find growth. It's in that beautiful tension that people around us are blessed with progress.

Don't be a neutered vanilla man. They aren't leaders. They frustrate marriages and homes. Stand up. Push hard. Take some risk. Bring a little excitement. Leading in that way often sucks, but that's the leadership our homes and our world need.

Want more?

Scan the QR code to check out more content by Junior. He has a bi-weekly email you can sign up for, a couple podcasts to subscribe to, as well as other books.

Junior Ziegler

Junior Ziegler

End Notes

[1] Steen, Ivan. "PHILADELPHIA IN THE 1850'S: As Described by British Travelers." *Pennsylvania History: A Journal of Mid-Atlantic Studies*, vol. 33, no. 1, pp. 30–49, https://doi.org/https://www.jstor.org/stable/27770385.

[2] Goheen, Peter G. "Industrialization And The Growth of Cities In Nineteenth-Century America." *Mid-America American Studies Association*, vol. 14, no. 1, 1973, pp. 49–63.

[3] Cox, Daniel A., et al. "American Men Suffer a Friendship Recession." *The Survey Center on American Life*, 7 Apr. 2022, www.americansurveycenter.org/commentary/american-men-suffer-a-friendship-recession/.

[4] Reeves, Richard V. "Of Boys and Men." Https://Ofboysandmen.Substack.Com/p/Why-Boys-and-Men, 10 Sept. 2022, Accessed 21 June 2023.

[5] Zablotsky, Benjamin, et al. "Prevalence and Trends of Developmental Disabilities among Children in the United States: 2009–2017." *American Academy of Pediatrics*, 1 Oct. 2019, publications.aap.org/pediatrics/article/144/4/e20190811/76974/Prevalence-and-Trends-of-Developmental?autologincheck=redirected%3FnfToken.

[6] Brueningsen, Christopher. "Boys in Crisis: Schools Are Failing Young Males. Here's What Needs to Change in Classrooms." *USA Today*, 10 Oct. 2021, www.usatoday.com/story/opinion/2021/10/09/boys-falling-behind-how-schools-must-change-help-young-males/5913463001/.

[7] Jacobson, Molly. "True Stories of the Oregon Trail." *OldWest*, 19 Jan. 2023, www.oldwest.org/oregon-trail-stories/.

[8] I Timothy 5:8

[9] "Kenner, La Weather Historystar_ratehome." *Weather Underground*, www.wunderground.com/history/daily/us/la/new-orleans/KMSY/date/1972-1-16. Accessed 29 June 2023.

[10] Landry, Tom. "Tom Landry Quote." *A*, www.azquotes.com/quote/553515. Accessed 29 June 2023.

[11] Kahloon, Idrees. "What's the Matter with Men?" The New Yorker, 23 Jan. 2023, www.newyorker.com/magazine/2023/01/30/whats-the-matter-with-men.

[12] Dean, Emily. "Dopamine, the Left Brain, Women, and Men." Psychology Today, www.psychologytoday.com/us/blog/evolutionary-psychiatry/201105/dopamine-the-left-brain-women-and-men. Accessed 6 July 2023.

[13] Sobel, Dava. "Galileo's Universe." *The New York Times*, 21 Nov. 1999, www.nytimes.com/1999/11/21/magazine/galileo-s-universe.html.

[14] "Galileo Galilei (1564-1642)." *British Journal of Sports Medicine*, Sept. 2006, www.ncbi.nlm.nih.gov/pmc/articles/PMC2564400/#:~:text=Being%20Professor%20of%20Mathematics%20at,he%20had%20received%20at%20Pisa.

[15] Salian, Neesha. "Give Your Brain a Rest: How Boredom Can Unleash Creativity." Gulf Business, 6 Nov. 2022, gulfbusiness.com/insights-how-boredom-can-unleash-creativity/#:~:text=According%20to%20researchers%2C%20boredom%20can,need%20to%20improve%20our%20lives.

[16] "How Family Dinners Improve Students' Grades." Educational Connections, 12 Nov. 2020, ectutoring.com/resources/articles/family-dinners-improve-students-grades#:~:text=Students%20who%20eat%20dinner%20with,relationships%20and%20healthier%20eating%20habits.

[17] Harter, Ronald. "Leadership Perspectives." *Pubs.Asahq.Org*, pubs.asahq.org/monitor/article-abstract/86/4/1/135918/We-Have-Met-the-Enemy-and-They-Are-Us?redirectedFrom=fulltext#. Accessed 19 July 2023.

[18] Carrillo, Sequoia. "U.S. Reading and Math Scores Drop to Lowest Level in Decades." *NPR*, 21 June 2023 www.npr.org/2023/06/21/1183445544/u-s-reading-and-math-scores-drop-to-lowest-level-in-decades#:~:text=U.S.%20reading%20and%20math%20scores%20drop%20to%20lowest%20level%20in%20decades&text=The%20average%20scores%2C%20from%20tests,are%20the%20lowest%20in%20decades.

[19] Hansel, Tim. *Holy Sweat*, Words Book Publisher, 1987, pp. 188–189.

Made in the USA
Monee, IL
04 January 2024

4d6cd437-b4da-436a-92c1-f029491aeea3R01